Amazon Fba 2021

The Most Complete Guide To Mastering The Art Of Retailing Products On Amazon for Beginners

Donald White

TABLE OF CONTENTS

INTRODUCTION

Being an "Amazon Seller" is a desire that many of our customers express and we have verified that it can give great satisfaction in terms of online sales.

Amazon Fulfillment, called Amazon Fulfillment (Amazon FBA: Fulfillment By Amazon) is a service offered by the marketplace. The solution is convenient and advantageous as it allows you to send your products to an Amazon warehouse where they will be stored, packed and shipped to the end customer.

The following in this article of mine is aimed at giving a first overview of FBA. So if you're interested in starting to understand how Amazon Fulfillment works (and I think you are, otherwise you wouldn't have bought this book) and making use of it, I think it can really help you.

Make good use of it, take advantage of everything you will find in this book, study and you will see that you will become the Amazon Seller you want to become!

Enjoy the reading!

Chapter 1 Creating Your Own Amazon Seller Central Account

Amazon Seller Central Account Checklist

There are a few details that you will have to provide when creating an Amazon Seller Central account.

Business Information
This field is related to contact information, business name, and address.

Email Address
You have to provide an email address that is suitable for such account. It should be already set up as well because Amazon will contact you immediately through the email.

Credit Card Information
Providing a valid debit or credit card is very important. If you offer details for an invalid one, Amazon will merely cancel your registration. The debit/credit card has to be linked to a valid billing address, too.

Phone Number
Since Amazon will also contact you back by phone during the registration process, you will have to provide a valid phone number you can be reached on.

Tax ID
GE

Security Number. During this step, you will be prompted to do the "1099-K Tax Document Interview."

State Tax ID

You will need to mention in which state or states you conduct your business to get the right state tax ID.

For the last two steps of the registration process, it is highly recommendable to consult a tax advisor or different websites like taxjar.com, avalara.com, and taxify.com.

Most Important Questions to Ask Yourself Before Creating an Amazon Seller Central Account

You should not set up the Amazon Seller Account without asking yourself a few questions.

1. Where you will send the Amazon order returns?

As mentioned before, Amazon is a company that's oriented towards customer satisfaction, and they are doing their best to improve the consumer experience on this platform. This also includes handling returns, considering customers can quickly return a product if they don't want it anymore due to different reasons. As a company selling on this platform, you will need to comply with this policy; that's why the return process is something you will need to consider. In other words, you will either need to care of it yourself or outsource it to an agency like tradeport.com or openedboxreturns.com. They specialize in grading and testing returns, as well as in placing the product on sale again.

Also, you have to think of a person from your company who can handle customer inquiries. Know that you not only have to answer everyone but also reply within 24 hours, regardless of the day of the year (according to Amazon's policy). Therefore, all these essential roles have to be figured out already before even creating the Amazon Seller's Account.

2. Is commingling an option if you choose to use Fulfillment by Amazon (FBA)?

The FBA option provides the seller access to a community of customers (Prime members), who spend more money on their Amazon purchases. This group has more than 100,000,000 members worldwide. However, you are not the only merchant who has access to this exclusive buyers club, given the fact that there are other 2,000,000 sellers in total on this platform, and the majority of them have access to the Prime members (Wallace et al, 2019).

Since you have to make sure that your products get to these customers, you can risk to mingle them with other merchants' goods, which may be the counterfeit versions of your items. The inventory is being sent to the fulfillment centers, where they might mix with the inventory of other sellers. A customer might receive a product as well which did not come from you, might be of lower quality, or even counterfeited. Hence, you have to provide serious explanations to the customer. If they file a complaint, you might also be banned from selling on Amazon, all because of a product which wasn't even yours in the first place. It now depends on you to prevent such thing from happening. When creating the Seller Account, it is "stickerless" by default, so you can commingle with other products from different inventories.

Fortunately, Amazon can give you the option of getting a "stickered" account but ensure to change the type of the account before sending the first shipment to the fulfillment centers. At least, this is the recommended way. You can also opt for the "stickered" selection later, but you might be exposing yourself to risks if you have already sent unlabeled inventory to Amazon.

3. Do you intend to use a Doing Business As (DBA) name for your Amazon Seller account?

This platform can allow you to hide your merchant identity from the customers by using a different name on Amazon. This is an option to consider if you don't want brands knowing that you are selling their products online, as well as when the reseller is the brand itself, and they don't want their partners to know that they do direct marketing on this platform.

4. Are your products in a category permitted by Amazon?

This is a crucial aspect as the FBA program doesn't allow all resellers to sell through some categories. E.g., alcoholic drinks, vehicle tires, gift cards, gift certificates and a few other products like pamphlets, sky lanterns or price tags. If you don't dabble in these things, then you're in luck because you can sell a wide variety of products without a hassle. Of course, it's highly recommendable for them to have a higher profit margin, but they should also be sold quickly.

Another fact that requires your attention is your seller catalog on Amazon. It's terrific to have all the goods added to your list within the first 30 days since the opening of your account. This way, you can easily find out if you will have problems with some specific stock keeping units (SKUs) and brands. In case they are inevitable, you may need to change your catalog or close the account, primarily if Amazon is imposing restrictions on the products you are planning to sell.

Must-Have Skills for Amazon Sellers

The Amazon marketplace is comparable to a wild jungle where only the strongest can survive. As a new seller, you have to be aware that there are 2 million other merchants like you on this website, so you have a stiff competition regardless of the products you are selling. To rise above everyone, you need to possess some skills and knowledge to boost your sales and always be in front of the game.

1. Outstanding marketing content to build the best product listings

There are high chances that others already sell the product you are selling on this platform. However, to make sure that your items come first, you will need to work on optimizing the details related to them. Focus on product title and description, bullet points, and generic keywords (for SEO purposes). Also, you should add very clear images, including the lifestyle photo of the product on sale. The main image needs to have a white background and a resolution of at least 500 x 500 pixels, but it's not necessary to place your brand on it.

2. Knowing how well your product is selling and how to prevent running out of stock

If you have a favorite product on Amazon, you need to be aware that you will eventually run out of stock. To avoid this scenario, you need to know how to replenish your inventory. Depending on the products that you usually sell, you can fill it again. If you are keen on selling one-time buys or close-outs, then you may have a tough time to replenish the stock since the products can be difficult to find again.

3. Choosing if you want to sell the same product or diversify

If you're going to trade one product on Amazon alone, you can benefit from some exciting tools like the alert and forecasting tools from Amazon. Alternatively, you may try getting help from the likes of www.forecastly.com.

4. Knowing how to find and deal with the old inventory

The truth is that some of the products may not be very popular and end up being stored for an extended period in the fulfillment centers. Such goods have to be sold on different selling channels to clear up the inventory in the warehouses since you might need to pay extremely high storage fees for them. The good news is that FBA can easily help you identify the old inventory, while the non-FBA programs force the seller to search by SKU to find the stale stock manually.

5. In-depth understanding of every cost

The majority of the sellers on this platform can understand the necessary expenses related to SKU - level profitability, which leads to an overall result - instead of having a clear idea regarding the SKUs that provide the highest profitability and the products that cost to sell on Amazon. Having a detailed cost situation can help the seller comprehend and put together the overhead expenses and acknowledge that those costs have to be integrated into the total amount.

Discovering who sells the same SKU on this platform

Without thorough research, you can end up listing your products on Amazon and discovering that there are plenty of other merchants with the same goods later. They will compete against each other to provide the best price for the product, which leads to low profitability or losses. Before creating the account, therefore, it is essential to find out if the products you are planning to sell are already massively sold on this platform, possibly even by Amazon Retail. If so, you will need to list different products on sale. Furthermore, it pays off to study not only your competition thoroughly but also their merchandise. If you are competing against sellers with low prices, you can't expect to have big profits in this niche. Then, you might realize that it may not be the best category to help you make money.

Furthermore, Amazon only charges a fee after the first 30 days of creating the account, so why should you not use that period to set it up properly? You can create the product offers and start selling to activate your sellable inventory, for one. Even if you don't send any listing to Amazon or sell anything, you can still be charged after 30 days because the account is active. In this period, you need to grow your business perspective on this platform. A good method to make it happen is to ask for feedback.

One of the options is to visit websites like feedbackgenius.com, feedbackfive.com, salesbacker.com, et cetera. They are not free of charge, but at least they are not expensive, so they are an investment worth taking. This strategy can show Amazon that the reseller can perform and comply with the platform's performance and customer- oriented policies.

Chapter 2 Creating Your Brand

While your first products are on their way to Amazon, it is a good idea for you to begin creating your brand. As you already know, your brand is key in helping you set yourself apart from other brands that already exist on Amazon. With your brand, you can create familiarity on Amazon itself, as well as on other platforms such as Instagram, Facebook, and Twitter, where you can drive traffic directly to your Amazon store.

If you chose to create private label products, you would want to have your brand already established *before* ordering them so that they are privately labeled with the right branding. For that reason, you should do this step before you officially purchase your products so that you can feel confident that they are going to match your branding.

In this chapter, we are going to explore all of the basics of launching a brand for your Amazon account, including how you can use other platforms to drive traffic to your website. You will also learn about how you can protect your brand to avoid having other Amazon merchants rip your brand off and potentially destroy your reputation and the credibility of your business along the way.

Choose Your Brand Identity

First things first, you need to choose your brand identity. Your brand identity is the identity by which you are going to be recognized, so you need to make sure that you choose one that is attractive and coherent. Your brand identity includes your name, your logo, your font, your colors, and your imagery. All of these factors are relevant in cultivating your brand, so make sure that you pay attention to all of them.

The name of your brand should be something relevant and catchy. It should make sense to your brand so that it is clear as to why you have chosen this name and what it represents. Ideally, your brand name should not be your own name, unless your own name is already popular and well known. Instead, choose a one or two-word brand name that represents what you are selling so that people will immediately recognize it and know who you are once you begin to establish brand familiarity.

Your logo and brand fonts should be the same, as you want to use your brand fonts in your logo. Typically, brands will choose two fonts that they are going to use to represent their brand. The first font is generally the header font that they are using, and the second font is the body font. These two fonts should go nicely together and should have a feel that is relevant to your industry. For example, if you are selling professional office products, you should use clean fonts like Arial or Helvetica. If you are in an elegant industry, choose something like a script header and a simple body font, such as Dancing Script and Arial.

You need to choose a few colors that are also going to represent your brand. Ideally, you should have three to four colors for your brand: one or two primary colors and then two secondary colors. Your colors are going to be used on everything from your labels to your graphics and everywhere else, so make sure they go well together and that they fit into your overall image. They should also be relevant to your industry by providing the right look and feel to your brand, as out-of-place colors can quickly make your brand seem unprofessional or misplaced.

Finally, you want to choose the actual imagery of your brand. Most brands will produce what is called a mood board, which is essentially a collection of graphics that give the feel for what your brand is going to offer. You might have people lying at the beach and sunsets if your brand is for lounging and relaxing, or you might have pictures of minimalism and fresh flowers if you want a minimalist eco-friendly appearance. Create whatever mood board you desire based on the look and feel that you want your brand to have.

Once you have put all of this together, lay it all next to each other to get a feel for what your final brand is going to be. This will give you an idea as to whether or not it works together and if it is going to provide the right look for your company. If you find that it does not perfectly reflect your brand, you are going to want to make a few adjustments to it so that it gives a better and more coherent feel for your customers.

Apply For Brand Registry

After you have created your brand, go on Amazon, and apply for a brand registry. You should do this before you do anything else with your brand as this is going to protect your brand from possible identity theft on Amazon. A brand registry can be applied for by going onto your professional seller account, heading to your settings, and selecting the "Brand Registry" feature.

In order to register your brand, you are going to have to provide the following information to Amazon:

- The name of your brand (it will need to be registered with U.S. Patent and Trademarks first)
- Brand serial number from your USPTO
- The countries where your products are manufactured and distributed by
  - Image of your brand name on a product that you will be selling
  - Image of your product label
  - Image of your product

Although this can take some time, it is worth doing so that you can protect your brand from being stolen by anyone else on Amazon. Remember, Amazon is an international marketplace, so having this added layer of protection is crucial in helping you avoid any unwanted brand identity theft that could take place.

As well, having this brand registration unlocks more branded features for you on Amazon, including the ability to brand your own storefront and product pages as per your brand's appearance. It is well worth the investment!

Brand Your Product Pages

Each time you upload products to your shop, you should be branding those pages. There are three areas of your product page that you want to brand in order to have your brand clearly displayed for your customers to see.

The first part of your product page you want to brand is your title. Your title can have up to 200 characters in it, so do your best to create a full title that features your brand's name, the title of the product, and anything else that someone may search when they are looking for your products.

The second part of your product page that you should brand is your product description. On Amazon's product pages, you can include up to 5 bullet points of information, with each bullet point containing up to 255 characters. Use these bullet points to provide clear information about what benefits people will gain from using the products and any search terms that they may be looking for when they are searching for products like yours. Refrain from making the bullet points spammy by listing search terms without any context, as this may actually reduce your rankings on Amazon's SEO, or search engine returns.

Finally, you want to brand your pictures. Your pictures should clearly display your product with your branded private label. You can also watermark your images with your brand name in the corner or somewhere along the edges, where it will not interrupt your image so that you can brand your product there as well. Each of your pictures should be relevant to your brand by having your brand's color scheme and mood artistically weaved into your picture. For example, if you have a fresh and clean eco-brand, you might photograph your product on a white background next to fresh green plants. If you have a rustic western brand, you might photograph your product on a wood background next to something like a vintage piece of furniture or decoration. Avoid going too crazy with your images; however, as cluttered images or images with too many decorations in them can be distracting and confusing. People may get overwhelmed with what they are looking at and may find themselves looking elsewhere instead of looking at your products because they simply do not know what they are looking at.

Brand Your Product Labels

In addition to branding your store, you also want to brand your product labels. Whenever you can, source products that allow for private labels so that you can label your products with your logo, fonts, and color scheme. Doing so is going to help you create products that are marketing your brand for you as they feature all of this information directly on them. Now, when someone buys your product, they are going to remember the brand it was purchased from, and they can use this information to buy more for themselves or to encourage their friends to buy something from you.

When you brand your product labels, try to stick to generally the same look on all products. Having the same background colors, imagery, and general design on your product labels will ensure that you are keeping your look uniform. This way, you are increasing your chances of having brand recognition because you are producing the same look every time. A great example of this is Coca-Cola. Their brand is represented by an iconic red with their scripted logo. Every time you look at a Coca-Cola product, you immediately know what it is because the branding is uniform and clear every single time.

Brand Your Amazon Storefront

On Amazon, after you register your brand, you are going to have the opportunity to brand your storefront. Your storefront is basically like your web store or your own private webpage on Amazon's platform that displays your products for sale. Branding your storefront is an important part of making it memorable so that people want to see it and pay attention to your products when they land on your page.

You can brand your storefront by choosing how many pages

you are going to have displayed on your store, what those pages are, and what categories they revolve around. You want to design your pages and categories in a way that reinforces the image and brand that you have already begun to develop so that when people land on your page, it feels like it truly belongs to your brand. In other words, *it makes sense.*

When you develop your storefront, a branded video on your front page that is about 30 seconds long is actually an incredible way for you to boost your viewership and your recognition. Although this will take more effort and time investment on your end, doing it can have a huge impact on your customers and can support you with increasing your sales numbers.

With your branded storefront, you can choose to have your own URL if you desire so that you can market both on Amazon's platform and off of it. If you really want to set yourself apart from the other brands on Amazon, this is a great feature. However, it is not necessary, so do not feel like you have to do this if you do not want to. You can still make plenty of money with your Amazon FBA platform without your own URL.

Brand Your Amazon Ads

However, it is important for you to know that this is a feature that is available to help you brand your business. Amazon offers three types of ads: sponsored product ads, sponsored brand ads, and sponsored display ads. Taking advantage of sponsored brand ads is a great way to promote your brand and help boost brand recognition so that you are more likely to make sales with your brand on Amazon. As well, sponsored brand ads provide you with the opportunity to show people what your brand is so that they can find your store and discover what products they are interested in, rather than having your individual products being marketed to them.

Brand Your Other Platforms

Once your Amazon brand has been built, brand your other platforms, too. With Amazon, you are not required to use social media to drive traffic to your store. However, it does help. Driving your own traffic to your own store by building a brand on social media and using that brand to funnel people increases your sales because it means you are no longer relying solely on Amazon's algorithm. You certainly do not have to do this, and if you do not want much involvement in this business you should skip this step, but if you really want to grow your store, this is an important step.

If you are on Instagram, Facebook, Twitter, or anywhere else on social media or the internet itself, make sure that you are branding your accounts. Use your logo in your graphics, choose graphics that are relevant to your brand, and create a brand that is going to help you establish recognition. Then, encourage people from your brand to find their way to your platform and purchase your products!

There are plenty of great books about branding on social media, so I highly recommend you grab one and use that as a part of your mindset growth and personal development if this is something you want to do. A book that is specifically designed around this topic will provide you with ample advice on how to brand each account and how to post in a way that accentuates your brand and gets your name out there in a bigger way.

Chapter 3 Creating Your Product Listing

Product Description

Having a well-crafted product description is important for having and optimized listing page. These are the key reason why it is crucial to have a great product description:

- A strong product description will convert shoppers into customers. More customers will create a better sellers rank which will allow your product to rank better organically. This will in turn create more sales without having to pay for ads.

- The product description is the main place to really highlight why your product is better than your competitors. In other words, this is the place to differentiate your product.

- Many other sellers do not fully utilize the product description, so this is where you can step in to capitalize on their laziness.

Product Description Details

There are some specifications of the description that you need to know:

- You are only allowed 2000 characters, not words!

- Basic formatting is possible - this includes basic HTML: bold, paragraph spacing etc.

Product Detail Tips

You should focus on writing your description as a sales letter, including a specific benefits, product guarantees and distinct call-to-actions.

Start with a catchy headline that will be certain to grab your customer's attention. Immediately give them a reason to buy your product rather than a product from a competitor. Really focus on your customer and how your product will benefit them.

Another great tip is to look at the positive and negative reviews of your competitor's products. See what people really like in other products and ensure that these features and benefits are strongly emphasized in your product description. On the other hand, if your product solves issues in other products that people have complained about, be sure to highlight these too.

You don't need focus on including all your keywords in your product description, although you will want to definitely include your top ones as this will help with ranking your product page on Google.

Here is a template to help your create an effective product description:

"Headline Sub-Headline Bullet point Bullet point Bullet point Benefits, Features, and Bonuses.

Guarantee and Call-to-Action!"

It can take up to 30 minutes for changes to appear on your Amazon product page.

Headline: Remember the headline needs to be attention grabbing. For example: "The Secret to Getting in Amazing Shape Without Going to the Gym".

Sub-Headline: Should be a strong continuation of the main headline.

Bullet points: This is where you can highlight the main features of your product. Highlight the advantages of your product! You can also include a bonus offer here.

Guarantee: Include strong guarantees as this significantly improves your conversion rate.

Call-to-Action: Tell your customers what to do! Remind them to buy your product now before shopping around.

If you follow this template for making an effective product description, this will really pay off by making your product stand out from your competitor's, and will drastically increase your conversion rate.

Using High Quality Images

In this section I will be covering why it is extremely important to use very high quality images on your product page. High quality images serve the following roles:

Drawing Attention - they grab a shopper's eye which will entice them to click through to your product over a competitor's. This is particularly important for the very first product image.

Stronger conversion rates - having a selection of high quality images gives a strong sense of professionalism and lets the customer really see and 'feel' the product. Needless to say, this really boosts your conversion rate. Having great images is the closest you can bring the customer to actually looking at a product in a physical store.

Product Image Specifications

- You are limited to 9 product images

- Your main image must have a white background - this is

Amazon's guidelines

- Your images should be at least 1000 pixels on the longest side - this allows customers to zoom in to your product.

  - Product Image Tips.

  - Make your first feature image very high resolution.

  - Always use the 9 images available for your product.

- Either hire a professional photographer to take your images or use your own or a friends high quality camera.

- You can then have these edited using a freelance website mentioned previously.

- Do not include promotional text or logos on your main product image - this is against Amazon's guidelines.

  - Get pictures of your product from all angles.

Overall, when it comes to selecting and uploading your product photos, make sure that your featured product image is superb. This is your best chance to put your product as close as possible to the customer's hands before they purchase it!

Other Details

In this section I will be explaining how to effectively fill in all of the other details in your product listing dashboard.

Search Terms

This is very important, and you can find this in the "Keywords' tab of the product listing dashboard. This is where you can use the keyword research that you did earlier. Simply plug in your top keywords into this section. This will help Amazon determine what customer searches to show your product for, so this is extremely important for getting your product in front of shoppers.

Product Dimensions

This is found in the 'More Details' tab and it is important to fill in as many details as you can. There will also be other fields that are not relevant to your products, but have a look to see what you can possibly fill in.

These details are not as important as your product description, but Amazon does prefer having as much detail as possible about your product which can help them get your product in front of more people.

Checklist of Required Actions

You're almost at the stage to launch your new product! Here is a checklist of actions that you must complete before starting on the next section:

- Conduct keyword research

- Create an effective title

- Highlight the features and benefits of your product in the bullet points section

- Create an amazing product description

- Get 9 very high quality photos for your product page

- Complete as many 'Other Details' in the product listing dashboard as you can

Chapter 4 Selling Fees

As you are sending your items off, be aware of the fees you will incur using the FBA service. Amazon does take a portion of the revenue you generate, but in the grand scheme of things, it usually pays to have this minor bit taken out. FBA fulfillment fees are constantly changing; you will need to keep a vigilant watch of the prices to notice how they fluctuate, usually around the time of the change in financial quarter.

Multi-Channel Fulfillment

The fees you are charged for using the FBA service depends on whether you are using only Amazon Fulfillment or Multi-Channel Fulfillment. Multi-channel fulfillment applies to sellers who are using other venues to sell their products, for example using an Etsy page or their own website. Sellers using Multi-Channel use Amazon as one way of directing traffic flow to their other selling channels. If you are interested in Multi-Channel fulfillment, you can look into this option for your business.

Fee types

Fees are applied to your items based on handling of the order, Pick and Pack, and the weight handling. This is why lightweight items can be particularly advantageous for your business. Fees are also applied differently for Media, Non-Media, and Oversized items. Non-Media items are classified in size tiers and also product type.

If you are selling an item over $300.00 worth in cost, you are able to sell it at no cost in terms of the fees leveraged against it.

FBA Revenue calculator

To learn more and calculate the fees that will be leveraged against your items, Amazon has made the FBA Revenue calculator available to its sellers. You need the following information to calculate the revenue you have the potential to earn on an item.

Item Price – what you plan to charge for the item.

Shipping – Because you are shipping through Amazon, they are taking over the fees, so this cost is assumed to be $0.

Order handling – this is determined by the type of item you are shipping and whether or not a flat rate exists for it.

Pick and pack – refers to the cost of the packaging materials necessary to ship your item to the warehouse. You will need to look at materials requirements established by Amazon for packing, which differ depending on the type of item. If you do not properly pack your items, you will be charged for this once they arrive at the warehouse.

Outbound shipping – with Amazon FBA, this is calculated as a flat rate depending upon the item.

Weight handling – Calculated using the scale specified by Amazon, with a special fee included for certain items, such as TVs.

Monthly storage – Charged by cubic feet of volume, differs monthly.

Inbound shipping – the cost of transporting your items to the Fulfillment center. If the items you are ordering have proper labeling, they can sometimes be sent directly to Amazon. This applies specifically to private label goods. With private label goods, your manufacturer can send the items directly to an Amazon warehouse if they meet Amazon requirements. Otherwise, you are responsible for shipping the goods.

Customer service – With FBA, the cost of customer service is already factored into your professional seller account, so there is no charge here.

Prep service – This applies if you opt for Amazon to fulfill your item prep and it is calculated per item.

Once you have inputted the above values, the Revenue Calculator will tell you the Referral cost and the Variable closing fee.

Storage fees

Amazon charges sellers a fee for storage, which is why it is critical to select items that sell well and quickly. Otherwise, you will be charged for the items that remain in storage. You are charged for the total cubic feet of your items.

The cost of the charge per cubic feet of your items varies depending on the time of year. Storage is more expensive in the latter half of the year due to the demands of the holiday shopping season. If your items sell slowly and are in storage for over 6 months or a year, depending on the item, you will be charged a long-term fee. This does not apply to single items; rather, the long-term storage fee only applies to items in bulk.

Before you get discouraged about the costs of shipping and handling, know that there is a key difference here between individual selling plans and professional selling plans. With an individual selling plan, an extra $0.99 is levied against the cost of your item in exchange for the FBA service.

Professional selling plans allow you as the seller to keep that

$0.99, preserving and strengthening your profit margin.

To avoid storage fees, keep the dates of inventory clean-up in mind. Amazon goes through its inventory on August 15th and February 15th; so as you are planning on dates to restock, consider how close you are to running into one of those dates.

| Monthly Recurring Revenue | ↑ 3.9% | Net Revenue | ↑ 7.7% |
| $1.26M | | $1.12M | |

Breakdown

| Fees | ↑ 8.5% | Other Revenue | ↓ 100.0% |
| $31,240 | | $0 | |

23 New

41 New S

23 Expan

| Average Revenue Per User | ↑ 1.0% | Annual Run Rate | ↑ 3.9% |
| $58.25 | | $15.1M | |

3 Reactiva

1 Contract

45 Churns

Total Change

| Lifetime Value | ↑ 16.2% | MRR Growth Rate | ↑ 33.7% |
| $997 | | 4.2% | |

Live Stream

● $29 paid by

● $149 paid by

● $29 paid by

● $29 payment

MacBook Pro

Search or type URL

Chapter 5 Your First Sales

One of the hardest parts of making decent earnings with online retail is picking the products you will be selling. For many, this can simply be things they find around their homes, at yard sales, garage sales, auctions, thrift stores, and other opportunities that arise. For others, especially those hoping to move in bulk, it is often better to find a reliable wholesale source. We will discuss that later in the book. For now, I want you to consider getting your toes wet first.

Sell Your Used Goods First

Before you go out and buy 1,000 beanie-babies to resell through Amazon's FBA program, let's take the time to get your toes wet and simultaneously declutter your home. Like most of us, I'm sure you have quite a bit of stuff in your house that you no longer need or want. This is a great opportunity to make some extra money while learning how FBA works. So dig out your closets, cupboards, storage spaces, etc., and set aside items that are in decent condition but are no longer any use to you. These are going to become your first shipments to Amazon. It is very easy to get started with just movies, video games, and books. Media items are great because they tend to sell well, the fees related to weight are low, and they are hard to really damage during a shipment.

From there, you'll want to make sure all your items are clean, in working condition, and that you've found a box large enough to ship your entire pile to Amazon. Since you're starting with items you already own, the profit is going to 100% even if it is a low profit. This is a great way to learn the ins and outs without making a huge purchasing mistake first.

To value your items, it is really as simple as making a list of everything you have, and checking each item against what is currently available on Amazon. Consider shipping as part of the overall price (customers will!), and write down the lowest price each item is available for on Amazon from other FBA sellers. (There will be a Fulfillmeny by Amazon logo telling you who the other FBA sellers are).

Using this list of items and prices, you should see that some items are simply not worth selling on Amazon. If you take a video game and look it up on Amazon to find that there are 10 sellers selling it for $0.01 in Like New condition, it's safe to say you can put that back on your shelf or donate it to a thrift store. There are other ways you could exchange them, such as used book/music/game stores, but most owners at these places are not going to give you much in return. However, even a lot of small $2-5 items are worth listing as you're getting your toes wet or if you are able to move a large enough quantity of items with high enough profits to justify the $40 per month that it costs to have a Pro Merchant account. Remember that you can use http://salecalc.com to get a better idea of what your items will ultimately bring you after all costs and fees are paid.

Setting Up Your FBA Account

Now that you have a pile of items and the prices you want to sell them for, it's time to actually get started on your adventure down the Fulfilment by Amazon road. Pick the first of these items you want to list, as you'll need an item to list to sign up as a seller.

If you have an Amazon account already, and you probably do, you can use this as your account for both selling and buying. Don't worry if you have a funny username. You will be prompted to choose a display name during sign up for a seller's account. If you don't have an Amazon account, now is the time to get one. Luckily, the process is simple and doesn't require much in the way of a tutorial.

Once logged into your account, you can click on your "My Account" link, which is typically going to be near the top right of the page. From this page, select "My Other Accounts." You should see a "Seller Account" link within the list; click on this and it will take you to the page with directions to setup a seller account on Amazon.

You will be prompted to sign up as an individual or a professional seller. We briefly discussed the paid, "Pro" program. For now, it probably suffices to use the "free" seller's account.

The next step is to list an item. Yes, you list an item before even finishing the rest of your seller's account signup. This should be fairly simple for you. You'll be asked what category you want to list an item in, and you'll be able to look your item up. If it is already for sale on Amazon, and it probably is, you should be able to select it from a list with thumbnails. Find the one that matches your product as close as possible. From here, you'll be asked to note the condition of the item. From the condition drop down menu, you can choose New, Like New, Very Good, Good, Fair, Poor, etc. Be honest about this. We'll discuss the different types of conditions you can choose shortly.

On the follow page, you'll be asked for a price. You should have this ready on your list. Next is your shipping method. Here you will be able to click, "I want Amazon to ship and provide customer service for my items if they sell." You will also be able to click a box saying that you want Amazon to remember this preference for new listings to come. There's no reason you can't sell and ship some of your items yourself and have Amazon handle others, though. Click the "continue" button, and Amazon will once again ask you to log into your account for security purposes.

The next page is where you will get to setup a display name. These will be displayed next to the listings that belong to your products, and the name should be something professional and approachable. You cannot have a display name that someone else has already used, so you may have to get a bit creative.

Accept the terms of agreement, and then let Amazon walk you through adding in your financial information, such as credit card. If you already have any credit or debit cards associated with your account, you will be able to select these from a menu. If not, you'll have to add a new card. Once this is done, you will be requested to verify your identify over the telephone by inputting your number and clicking "Call now!" You should get a phone call within a minute, and a verification number should appear on the screen. This number will be given over the phone to the automated system, and after a short minute on the phone, you should be allowed to continue with your setup on Amazon as a seller. (NOTE: This financial information is for YOU to make payments to AMAZON in the event that your seller account goes in the negative or you sign up for other services. It is NOT the setup for getting payments. We will cover that later.)

The next step is to review your listing and approve it. Because you've opted for Fulfillment by Amazon, your item will not go up for sale immediately. Instead you'll be asked to agree to Amazon's terms of services once more and then prompted to "Get started with Fulfillment by Amazon." This will bring you through a number of video tutorials that you can watch. I advise that you take the time to watch them at some point, even if you don't do so right away.

At the bottom, you will be able to click a button that says, "Send items to Amazon." You will not immediately have to ship anything to them, but it will ask if you want to ship "stickerless" items or "Stickered" items. "Stickered" inventory consists of used items that will require a sticker barcode generated by Amazon to be sold through the FBA program. You can pay Amazon to sticker your items for you if you wish, but keep in mind that this raises your costs. "Stickerless" items must be new items that have a product barcode on them. "Stickerless" items are "co-mingled" with the same items from other sellers. Because these items are all brand new, Amazon can simply store them together and ship any of them out regardless of the actual seller, which in turn means less storage costs. You may want to take advantage of this down the road, just be sure not to apply it to your used items. That won't work. We will cover stickering in more detail later, so keep this concept in mind.

From here, you'll be asked once again if you want your item to be fulfilled by Amazon. Allow this, and on the following page do not click "convert" or "convert and send." You will do this later, once you've stocked your inventory and prepped your shipment. Your item(s) will simply sit in your inventory as inactive until you're ready.

Your seller account is technically ready to go. The next step is listing the rest of your products.

Listing Products

The one part FBA won't cover for you is listing all of your items. You still have to take the time to build each listing, write a brief description, add images if you choose, and add a price. The process is simple, but it can be time consuming if you're selling a lot of items individually (rather than in large quantities).

First, pull up your list of items (whether it's on paper or in Excel) and start from the top. I suggest having a column in your list that helps you realize what has been listed already and what hasn't, just in case you aren't able to list all items in one sitting. The easiest method to find your product is probably to type the product name in the search bar at Amazon.com, and find the product that best fits the item you're selling. From here, you should see a "Have one to sell?" link at the top-left area of the page.

Alternatively, you can use the inventory section on your seller's dashboard by selecting the link that reads, "Add a Listing" under the "Inventory" menu. The search engine that appears here will allow you to attempt to find what you're selling. If the product has some sort of identification number, this is the ideal method to find what you are selling. This is especially common on books with ISBNs and barcodes. Some items will not have an identification number or any type of barcode, though, and you'll have to simply try your best to find the one that matches your product. Keep in mind that you have a small description box where you can add notes should you place a product in a listing that isn't a 100% perfect match, especially if color is the only difference. Try to always disclose this information.

On the following page, you'll be prompted to input text regarding almost all the information on the product that you could possibly need to include. The form is easy and simple to follow, and it takes no time to setup your listings. The only reason it is time consuming is because you're going to be selling hundreds of items and making killer profits in no time. Let's discuss some of the fields.

SKU:

One of the fields will be for an "SKU." This number is intended to help with keeping your inventory in order. It is highly advised that you create a SKU for everything, especially items that you need to sticker later. Because Amazon creates SKUs randomly if you don't do so manually, letting them handle the SKUs themselves is almost always going to be a headache since the stickers don't always print in the correct order of how you've organized them. I would use a five-digit code and start your first product off as 00001 and move forward from there. Keep a note about which number you last used, as SKUs cannot be repeated, and the next time you list items, you'll want to start where you left off to help keep everything proficiently organized.

Condition:

The next item is a drop down menu that lets you pick the condition of your item. There are several types of conditions to choose from.

NEW – An item that has never been used whatsoever. For items that come sealed, this means the item is still sealed. For items that don't come sealed, this means absolutely perfect condition. If it comes in a box, the box should be included.

USED – LIKE NEW – In near-perfect condition. Should be as a new looking as an item that's never been used.

USED – VERY GOOD – Clean items with only very minimal wear.

USED – GOOD – For items that have scuffing or small imperfections, the "Good" condition is ample. Any imperfections should be purely cosmetic. An item must function 100% to be considered in "GOOD" condition.

USED – ACCEPTABLE – Clearly not in the best of condition but still fully functional, such as a used text book with highlighter in it.

With all of these conditions, you'll be able to leave a note regarding condition and any other details you may wish to portray. Try to be thorough and honest when choosing conditions and leaving notes. A simple note saying, "Highlighted text, but fully readable," is suitable.

It's important to understand that people are willing to buy things in less-than-perfect condition if they still work well, so lying about this isn't really helpful anyway. On the other hand, if an item is poorly categorized within these conditions or the notes suggest something that isn't true, you are more likely to see items being returned or your seller account getting poor feedback from buyers.

You will see that some sellers simply use the same bit of text on the condition note over and over. While this is a great way to cut back on time-consuming tasks, it is often misleading and not helpful to the potential customer. Take the time to write these in. It only takes a few seconds to determine the quality of your product.

Price:

The next part should be easy, but that isn't always the case. You should have already put together a list of prices when sorting and valuing your items. Remember, the number you should write down is the lowest available price from another Fulfilled by Amazon seller. In this section, Amazon will provide you with the lowest price for your item. There is the option to "MATCH" these low prices. Never. Ever. Use. This.

The problem with using price matching to price items is that the cheapest one available for your item could be a destroyed mess where yours is practically new. Additionally, you must remember that those selling FBA are your direct competition, not every seller on Amazon. So it really pays to go to the product listings and see what the competition actually looks like. There's no reason you need to sell your Like New item for less than an item covered in dirt and grime, or something far worse.

Instead, you should be pricing your items based on their condition and what you believe people will pay for it. The lowest price isn't always the item that sells, and sometimes we cannot sell items as cheap as other providers without losing money. In the end, you can always adjust your price later if it seems like an item might sell better at a different price point. On the same note, pushing for the lowest price is likely only going to force other sellers to lower their prices, driving down the perceived value of your item even further.

If you have a rare or expensive item, don't be tempted to way undercut the only other listing. If there's a listing for a rare item priced at $200, listing yours at $100 only works to drive down the market value. Instead, you should price competitively without undercutting the value of the item; anything else is just counter-productive. Some rare items may be worth a lot but only have a limited number of interested buyers. In these scenarios, you may just have to wait for the item to finally sell or consider another selling method.

Again, keep in mind that your competition isn't as broad as a seller that isn't using Fulfillment by Amazon. Because you're allowing them to ship your items, shoppers with Prime membership perks and those looking to score free shipping on orders over $49 are more likely to buy your items even if they aren't quite as cheap as the lowest available in the same condition. Use this to your advantage when pricing, because your most direct competition is only other listings that are using FBA.

When it's possible, being the only seller that is working through Fulfillment by Amazon is going to be a great advantage. Some people will even take the time to locate popular items without any sellers using FBA, and because they can offer the perks that others aren't offering, that item can usually sell quicker and for a little more money.

Keep in mind that it doesn't matter too much if the product is cheaper on another website. Your competition is within Amazon, not with the entire world wide web. So even if you find the same product for half the cost, if the lowest on Amazon is higher, you can still price within that range. You might even considered buying the item from another site if it's cheap enough for you to make a profit.

Setting the price can be the easiest or the hardest part of working for yourself through FBA, and it's important not to be lazy and simply list at the lowest possible at all times.

Quantity:

The next item on your product listing form is the quantity of the item you are selling. Even if you have multiples of the same items and the condition is not the same, Amazon will require you to list them together. This is unfortunate because it makes it difficult to be totally transparent and almost forces you to list a like new item as something less than like new.

Restock Date:

Unless you intend to restock the same items over and over, leave this field blank. This is only useful if you restock on a regular basis.

Other Fields

There are other fields sometimes related to the category. For example, a book listing will allow you to add in information concerning the country of publication. These should all be self-explanatory or easily searched when you're unsure. Often, you will/can simply ignore these optional questions either way.

Shipping Method:

Lastly, you will enter the shipping method you wish to use. There will be an option for having Amazon fulfill the order. This is what you will likely check.

Images:

Likely we've already passed this section, but one thing worth noting is that if there are no stock images available (and even if there are), it may be a good idea to add images to your listing or even submit them to the main listing so the item doesn't have a "no image shown" icon. This is important because images help buyers make a connection with a product before they purchase it. Most people don't want to purchase an item they can't see. If you have the patience and time, or if you only stock a handful of items, you may want to invest in the effort of taking photographs for all of your listings. These can greatly help to increase sales.

Save and Finish

Once everything is entered, you will click on "Save and Finish" to complete your listing. You will be given the option to "Send Inventory" or "Go Back." You will want to click "Send Inventory."

Add to Shipment

Following submitting your first product, you will be asked to confirm your address and add your item to a shipment. Since you don't have a shipment setup yet, your option will be to "Create a New Shipment." Click this and start a shipment. As you continue to list products, you will have the option to join them into an existing shipment in many cases. In some cases, you may not be able to do this and will be required to open a new shipment.

Take a moment to understand this faucet of FBA. Not all items can be sent to the same fulfillment center at once. As such, as you create shipments, you may be forced to ship several different bundles of items to multiple locations.

In your inventory, you may notice that there is a four-digit code next to your items. This code represents the fulfillment center appropriate for the item. Since not all items go to the same fulfillment centers, you may be working on shipping several boxes at once. Try to make sure you're keeping this stuff organized correctly. Do not completely pack your items yet, as we'll need to add the SKU stickers first. It is wise, however, to place them in a box to get an idea of the total weight of your package. Write down this weight when you're finished.

After listing your last item and choosing to add it to a shipment or create a new shipment, you will have the option to "Save and Continue" on this same page. Do this only once you've listed all your items! If you need to list another item, click the "Home" link and repeat the process above. Otherwise, you may be wasting money shipping small packages when you could send out only a few large ones and help keep down your operation costs, or have to deal with the headache of canceling and adjusting.

Chapter 6 How and Why to Private Label!

There are several different ways to sell products on Amazon. One of the most popular ways is through retail arbitrage where sellers visit retail stores (they spend HOURS in there or visit their online stores) and find items that are heavily discounted to buy them in BULK (or at only a few units at a time) and then go on to sell them for a profit on Amazon after packaging and sending in the products themselves. Retail arbitrage is a great way to get started in the business of selling on Amazon as you learn the ropes and get hands on experience with it but unless you simply don't have the capital for private label we would say just start with private labelling as you will eventually get to it if you're any part successful at retail arbitrage. Another common way of selling on Amazon is through buying products from wholesalers. This process called wholesaling is where sellers buy established products cheaply through established wholesalers and then send and list these products on Amazon. Another way people get into selling on Amazon which isn't as common is when they are already selling products through their own stores or business and decide to make them available on Amazon.

One of the most lucrative strategies for selling on Amazon is private labeling. Private labelling is generally considered the apex of selling when it comes to Amazon as it is the most complex (and by complex that simply means it has more steps to it than the other methods do). With retail arbitrage and wholesaling, the products you sale are generally not sustainable over the long term. The issue with retail arbitrage is that you need to keep finding products that are heavily discounted and in stock, this takes up a lot of your time and doesn't result in a true passive income stream. A lot of people are doing retail arbitrage as well so then retail arbitrager's start getting into price listing wars with each other on Amazon. This kills what little profit margins they had to begin with and there are other issues such as getting product listings hijacked etc., which is a whole other topic on their own. With wholesalers, anyone can find the same wholesaler and decide to purchase the products from them and start reselling on Amazon. This results in a loss of sales and will most likely turn into a price war as well, with profit margins decreasing once more. It isn't quite true that private labelling is the apex of selling on Amazon because once you are brand and sales are really established, you have the opportunity to then start wholesaling your product (so people will be coming to you to buy your product in bulk to sell) and also look for opportunities to get your product into retail stores making the circle whole. This comes up a lot later down the track so it's nothing that you need to concern yourself with.

With private labelling however, you pay a manufacturer (or a reseller of a manufacturer if you're not careful!) to produce items straight from their factory line and they slap your own private label to the products. From there you *can* have the factory package and label the products and deliver the products directly to Amazon's warehouses or if you would prefer, you can choose to send your products to companies based in the US who will then do the packaging and labelling for you before shipping it off to Amazon. From here you put up a product listing on Amazon which will include the product description, photos, and other similar details such as dimensions, weight and so forth. When your shipment lands in Amazon's warehouse, begin marketing and execute the launch phase for the product. Sit back, relax, and monitor sales.

Private label selling is nothing new in terms of business and it's likely you've bought private label products frequently in the past. Many generic items in supermarkets may be produced from the exact same source: the value brand milk you buy at Walmart and Costco may have come from the same cow at one point in time. Some supermarkets may even sell the same product within their own store. It's just that the exterior in terms of the branding, labeling, and packaging are different. More blatant attempts of this are evidenced in independent discount stores that might, for example, sell the exact same bottle of superglue only with different packaging or labels. These identical products may even be involved in pricings wars between the respective brands that sell them.

Amazon has actually taken hold of the private label game as it sells an entire range of items with its own logo and label. Fortunately though, this kind of private label selling is open to you as well. Whereas before you might have only sold such products to independent stores, you can now sell directly to a large mass of consumers by using Amazon as a platform. FBA provides a unique opportunity because it gives you the tools to research different markets, identify what is popular, and what is not so popular, and it gives you a place to list an item where customers are already looking for similar products and are willing to spend their cash. What you first need to do is pick the correct product, fill a need in the product's market and supply it to the horde of consumers. So enough with the frivolities, let's get down to the real meat and guts of this business and what you purchased this book for!

Chapter 7 Amazon FBA Seller Pricing and Repricing Tools

Determining how much to sell a product becomes easy with the use of pricing and repricing tools. These are used by sellers to list, scout and reprice products.

To begin with, let's consider Amazon's native app.

Amazon Seller App

Amazon has now created its own seller app to help Amazon sellers. The Amazon Seller mobile app can make your life easier as an Amazon seller to instantly update your FBA inventory, find and list new products online and answer customer inquiries.

The following are the Amazon Seller app features that make this app useful:

Update Inventory - Easily manage your Amazon FBA inventory: You can find, sort and filter product items, update your selling prices and change item quantities quickly from your mobile phone.

Source New Items to Sell - By entering product names or scanning barcodes, you can now compare existing selling prices, product sales rank and the customer reviews of the specific products on Amazon.

Calculate The Potential Earning of Products Before Selling - Add product price information to find out the expected potential earning of products.

List New Products to Sell - Make new product listings on Amazon instantly and conveniently.

Respond to Customers Inquiries - Give impressive customer support by replying quickly to customers inquiries.

View your current earnings - See how much earnings you currently have and when you'll get paid by Amazon.

Get Assistance from Amazon - Use the app to get in touch with seller assistance using email or chat.

Download the Amazon Seller App: If you want to try the Amazon Seller app, you can download it for free. You can get it from Google Play for Android, Apple for iOS and also from the Amazon App Store if you are using an Amazon device.

Choosing which seller app to work with is solely based on personal taste and preference. In some cases, there are some important features that you can get from non-Amazon apps. However, it will require you to spend more. If you are just okay with that, you can find out below which app can work best for you and your budget.

1. Listing Tools

Listing of products through the Amazon Seller Central can be time-consuming especially if you'll be listing more than 50 items a month. Listing tools are used to automate and speed up the process of putting up your inventory on Amazon.
ASellertool - This allows you to batch large quantity of items all at once and it supports FBA shipment management and label printing. You can register the Amazon Batch Listing software after registering your Amazon MWS (Marketplace Web Service) account to Asellertool service.

Listtee - This tool offers a simple listing software that links to all US and UK Amazon FBA warehouses. With this tool, you can replenish items and print single labels. It also has a feature on SKU detection to avoid listing of the same item twice, thus reduce listing errors.

Neatoscan - This tool is used to sell on multiple platforms. If later on, you decide to sell aside from your Amazon Seller account, then you may try the Inventory Manager tool. This tool integrates your online business so you can save time and costs while increasing productivity. The features include prescanning and receiving, inventory management, shipping, reports and FBA integration.

2. Scouting Tools

Getting a good product should be your main goal whenever you want to list an item on Amazon. To help you make wise decisions about potential inventory, you can use scouting tools. Most of the listing tools are integrated with its scouting tool so that after scouting, the listing could be easy and quick to accomplish.

Asellertool FBA scan - This App is for Android or iPhone gadgets, which can help you in checking the Amazon pricing information by scanning or entering the item's barcode. One good advantage of this App is that it has two scouting modes, the Local Database, and Live Search. The former requires no internet connection or can be used in areas with poor signal wherein the price information is stored in your phone, while the latter is used with internet connection and get real-time Amazon price information including those not found in local databases.

Listtee Scout Rabbit - This App can be availed from Listtee Pro and Enterprise Lite plans. It is another App to bring you the basic FBA pricing data as well as sales rank across all Amazon categories. When scouting for items, product barcodes can be read by Bluetooth scanner, a phone camera and by typing the name of the product.

Neato-scan – Neato-scan has another tool, the Neato-pricer. This tool utilizes a barcode scanner and PDA or iPhone/Android device without a need for internet connection. This helps you to have a quick and easy way to determine the value of the merchandise. It requires you to download first the PDA before you scan all categories.

- **Seller-Engine Profit-bandit App** - This App is considered as the #1 mobile Amazon seller software, which is downloaded either for iPhone or Android phones. Profit Bandit is a tool that helps seller maximize profit, keep an eye on the competition, and save time while making money. Using this App will help you find how much profit you can make from the item you want to sell. It scans the barcode and computes the cost including the FBA fees and you'll get the possible profit.

Scan power Scout - This App provides a real-time data from Amazon and access to the entire catalog. A very useful App because of the information it provides that include data of other FBA sellers such as the number they are selling and the net price after taking out Amazon fees.

- **Scout-pal** - There are two tools that can be used from Scout-pal: the Instant Lookups with a PDA and Live Lookups with a phone. The tools are simple and easy to use whenever you scout for items. You only need to enter the ISBNs or UPCs of an item and the tool will get the information you need. If you have a scanner attached to your device, you can scan it instead of entering the data. Then, you'll see information on the lowest prices in used/new/collectible lists, Amazon price, and sales rank. More so, the Live results will show the market prices and quantities, editions and availability. To easily comprehend the report, you can customize the content and format the details according to your preference.

•

3. Repricing Tools

With a dynamic marketplace such as the Amazon, updating and keeping your inventory with the right price is necessary. Repricing tools help you automate the process by selecting your criteria and reprice a large number of items within a short amount of time. Most of the repricing tools are offered with a listing tool such as the Neato-Scan Inventory Manager; it is advisable that you evaluate every part of the features and go for the best App for you.

Reprice-It - This tool is a cloud-based system, thus, no software needs to be downloaded. You can access your account anywhere with internet connection. This tool allows you to schedule repricing more frequently during peak buying times on Amazon while experimenting with different repricing strategies. Most importantly, this tool has full FBA support and you'll get detailed repricing reports onto your email.

Scan-Power -This App is used by sellers when listing items to sell. It has different features like Evaluate and Reprice for great use of sellers. These features help you calculate the prices based on FBA net price, which includes the price and shipping.

Sellery - This tool from Seller-Engine is used to help sellers compete and maximize profits. It features the Sellery's on-demand, per item pricing preview where you can create new pricing rules, pick any item in your inventory and preview your pricing strategies. With this App, you can prevent price mistakes because floor price calculation is automated and item-specific. It includes Amazon fees, FBA and shipping costs aside from the margin you want so you can come up with an accurate minimum price.

Amazon FBA Tools are definitely a must-have on your phone when you start selling on Amazon. An extra fee for the Apps will ensure that you are pricing your items properly and competitively on Amazon. No need to guess any price for your item. If you want to get the highest possible margin for your inventory, make sure that your pricing is calculated based on accurate data and information.

Materials Needed For Your Shipment

Starting out selling on Amazon will require a few materials that are needed in order to send your products to an Amazon warehouse. Some tools are very necessary while others will just make your life as a seller easier. Investing in tools that will increase productivity is a great idea and should be considered.

1 - Boxes

Let's begin with materials that are necessary. We're going to need shipping boxes. For your first shipment I recommend you collect free boxes from anywhere you can get them such as local stores, Craigslist and friends are all good options. Once you begin sending more and more shipments are required then buying boxes would be a better idea. All home improvement stores sell boxes that are perfect for FBA. Try and stick with small or medium boxes and only use large boxes if your shipment will be bulky.

2 - Packing Tape

Packing Tape and a Tape Gun are going to very important tools to pack your boxes together. You can buy these anywhere and at a cheap price. If you start shipping out more boxes then consider buying tape in bulk instead of single rolls. The minimum tape size that you should use is 2.2 mil. However, those tapes that are bigger and larger will stick better on the box.

3 - Measuring Tape

You need to measure the boxes you are about to send out to Amazon. Every box needs to be measured before you print a shipping label. You can get an inexpensive measuring tape at your local thrift store. Many retail stores have some affordable ones.

4 - Printer

The Dymo Label Printer is perfect for FBA labels and you will save money since you won't be buying ink anymore. However, for starters, you can use a toner laser printer since their prints don't smudge.

For the complete printing and labeling information, please see Amazon's printing guidelines.

5 - Labels

For printing your product label barcodes, you will need a standard 30-up address label. I highly recommend the Avery 18160 and 5160 address labels. However, you could also find other generic address labels that will work as good as the branded one.

If you don't want to spend more money, printing your barcodes on a white blank sheet of paper and using a tape to stick them on the boxes, can work as well. However, the time and effort for you to do it yourself are not so worth it. Address labels are just cheap, just buy them and save yourself from trouble.

Just make sure your labels are printed and placed properly on your boxes or products.

To learn more about proper labeling, please view this YouTube tutorial by Amazon: How to Label Products for Fulfillment by Amazon.

6 - Scales

Shipping scales are going to be needed to accurately calculate the weight for your boxes. At first using a bathroom or a kitchen scale will work fine but I highly recommend a shipping scale to properly weigh your products.

7 - Poly Bags

Consider as well having the poly bags since you will need to put many of your products enclosed with poly bags.

With these items, you will have what is needed for shipping. It may be a little costly at first but these are only initial investments that will surely pay off in the long run. Always remember to follow all of Amazon's rules and regulations.

How To Ship Inventory to Amazon Fulfillment Centers

In this section, I will discuss more how to ship products to Amazon, since they are the ones who will handle individual shipping to buyers. All we have to do is send our products to the Amazon warehouse.

Before we ship anything to Amazon we need to make sure our products are packaged and labeled. We cannot just send them products with no encasing so make sure your product packing is secure. Once the items are ready then we are going to have to pack them into boxes to be shipped to Amazon. Make sure to print shipping labels for your boxes that can be found in the Inventory section that will include a list of products within the box and the quantity.

It is very advisable to use as few boxes as possible to avoid any possible loss. Furthermore, make sure to protect your products when packing with foam, air pillows or sheets of paper. Finally, check the boxes to see if they are sealed and your products will not move during shipping. When it comes to choosing a carrier you are free to choose any carrier with any shipping speed you wish. Just make sure to provide the tracking numbers when using your own carrier.

As mentioned before, make sure to print shipping labels for all your boxes. Go to the Shipping Queue to print them out and attach the labels to the outside of the box. The labels will show the destination address and return address. In some cases, the tracking number can also be shown, if you are using an Amazon carrier. This will make sure that all your products are packaged for protection against any damage during shipping or storage and that all units follow Amazon's labeling and requirements.

When a product is shipped out to a customer your name does not appear on any item labels nor shipping labels but on the packing slip that will be found inside the box. This is the only reference the buyer has that the product came from you.

Amazon also accepts shipments from other countries to their warehouses. However, the seller will have to arrange the imports of his product, go through customs and lastly get the products delivered to an Amazon warehouse. Amazon will not serve as an importer for your imported products, they will not take responsibility for any taxes or fees related to your import nor will they provide a tax number for you. The seller is responsible for dealing with all government agencies that relate to his import and has to provide prepaid delivery to the Amazon warehouse. Also, Amazon does not provide any quality check to your products unless they are obviously and visibly damaged. If the item is labeled as "used" then it is understandable that it may have minor damages and will not be checked.

Dealing with customs, shipping charges, and all the different taxes is a total problem. Fortunately, there are many companies, referred to as freight forwarders, which could handle everything on your behalf. You simply connect your forwarder with your manufacturer and they can get all the details taken care of.

You can check the following freight forwarders and their services and see which one can best satisfy your requirements:

- <u>Forest-Shipping</u> - *Frequently Asked Questions for FBA shipment*
- <u>Riversource-Logistics</u> - *How It Works, Support Center*
- <u>Adstral-Fulfilment</u> - *Amazon Fulfillment*
- <u>Shapiro</u> - *Amazon FBA*
- *FBA-forward* - Services
- **AMZ**-transit - **Services**

Once again, Amazon does its best to make selling as easy as possible. All you have to do is get your products to the warehouse in good condition while following the requirements set by Amazon and we will be good to go.

How Amazon Handle Returns and Warranty?

Returns are common in this business. Maybe the buyer expected your product to be different, possibly damaged due to everyday reasons or they decided they just don't want your product anymore. Don't let it affect the way you feel about your product nor the way you conduct business. As long as you are keeping returns at a minimum then you're doing just fine.

With that said, we must know how to handle returns and the procedures that come with them. Amazon has always made it easy for its customers when it comes to return, they will process the whole return. Once the product reaches Amazon they will determine if the product is eligible for return or not. They will however usually accept units if they are returned within a certain time frame.

When the customer is issued the returned then Amazon will charge your seller account for the product including any taxes in order to reimburse the returnee. Now if the product is damaged and is found unsellable then Amazon will reimburse you, this also applies if the item was lost or never arrived at the buyer.

The Customer Return Timeline for most products is 30 days and 90 days for Baby products. For products that are returned within the timeline, they will firstly have the product checked for any damage that would make the product unsellable. Products that are still in sellable condition will be placed back into your inventory in the warehouse. While any products that appear to be damaged will not be placed back into your inventory and you will be fully reimbursed for the item. There are certain cases where

Amazon will not take responsibility and you will not be reimbursed for the item.

Amazon will always consider all cases that are returned outside the return timeline and from time to time accept returns. If Amazon decides to accept the return then the same procedure would be followed as if the item was returned within the timeline, you will be fully reimbursed as well.

Let's go over what makes an item sellable or unsellable. An item that is still sellable will be added back to your inventory while any items that are considered unsellable will be placed in your "Unfulfillable Inventory" if Amazon in certain cases does not reimburse you. An item is unsellable if it is not in the same condition that it was originally shipped as or if the product is opened, damaged, defective or special cases when Amazon finds your product unsuitable.

Amazon once again shows how they take care of everyone working with them. Returning is made easy for the buyer and the seller. Just remember that returns are part of being a seller so get through them smoothly and continue selling.

Chapter 8 Driving Traffic to Your Product

By now you should have your product listing page built and your products on the way to the fulfillment center or waiting there ready to be sold! In this section I will be covering the most effective ways that you can start driving traffic to your product to make your initial sales. It's time to start making money!

Website & Blog

Although your product is selling on Amazon, there are a bunch of reasons to build a separate website for your brand and product:

• Helps build your brand

• Makes your company look very professional

• Allows you to further communicate with your customer base

• *Allows you to collect email addresses from customers* Within your website you can build a blog which has numerous benefits, such as ranking in Google for your topics and placing you as an authority in your niche.

There are a variety of companies that you can use to start a website, but here are the key things that you will need to start:

• Website domain for your brand

• HOSTING

• Word Press

• *Basic or premium theme*

This should all cost less than $100, which is a small price to pay for the benefit that it can have for your brand and product. Ultimately, this will help drive traffic to your Amazon product and increase brand awareness.

Amazon Ads

The best way to start immediately driving traffic to your product is by using Amazon Sponsored Ads. This is the easiest and quickest way to start generating revenue for your new business. These ads are shown throughout the Amazon search pages, and you will be charged for these ads on a cost- per-click basis. You do not create the ads yourself because the ad information taken directly from your product page.

Auto vs. Manual Campaign

There are two types of campaigns that can be set up, but it's important that you only run one at a time. Auto campaign:
With an auto campaign you don't have control over the keywords being targeted or the cost per click for each keyword. I recommend using this type of campaign in the initial stages because it will give you keywords that you might not have thought of and may make sales from. You can then target these keywords within a manual campaign.

Manual campaign:

After running an auto campaign I strongly recommend running a manual campaign which will allow you to target specific keywords and have more control over your cost-per-click and overall ad spend. You can use the keywords that you discovered in your initial keyword research and ones discovered when running the auto campaign.

Setting Up Your Amazon ads

- Login to your Amazon Seller Central account.

- Go the 'Advertising' tab in the menu bar.

- Click on 'Campaign Manager'.

- Click on 'Create Campaign'.

- Enter your campaign name, I recommend using the product name.

- Set your daily budget - something you are initial comfortable with, I recommend starting at around $15 per day to begin with.

  - Add a start date.

  - Select your targeting type - Auto or Manual campaign.

  - Click 'Continue to the Next Step'

  - Create an Ad Group

  - Select the product you want to advertise.

- *Select a default bid based on the average winning bid.* Once set up, your ads can be live within 30 minutes - you can start making sales that very day!

Optimizing Amazon ads: If you see a keyword getting a lot of clicks but little sales, it is probably best to either reduce the bid on this keyword or even remove the keyword if it is performing very poorly.

Ideally, you should be able to run ads that are profitable, and this is the result of selling products at a slightly higher price point. Remember to keep optimizing and improving in order to improve your cost of ads per sale. Keep running your ads even if you are only breaking even - the more sales you make, the higher Amazon will rank your product in the search results. This will allow you to make organic sales without ad spend in the future.

Other Methods of Driving Traffic

- Search engine advertising on Google and Bing

- Press releases

- Facebook ads

- Pinterest ads

- Coupon and deal sites

Chapter 9 How to Get Ungated in Restricted Category?

A lot of bundles that are sold on Amazon through FBA include health products, groceries and beauty products. These products are restricted to be sold by approved sellers. You can still make your own bundles by combining products listed in ungated categories- baby products, housewares, garden and lawn products, kitchenware, and many more.

However, if you are not an approved supplier for health and beauty, groceries, etc.; you can still utilize the great opportunity to apply for the same. You can get approved in these categories easily.

You can sell millions of products from your Amazon Seller Account. But, some products fall in the restricted category. This is done by Amazon to control the sale of inferior quality products by sellers through their website. You can overcome most of these restrictions if you have good quality products to sell, while many other restrictions are not easy to overcome.

Restricted Categories

The gated or restricted categories can be overcome by taking permission from Amazon to sell your goods in these categories. Most sellers would just keep away from these gated categories assuming that they need to be a huge company to sell in these categories. But in actuality, the process of application is really uncomplicated. You would not face any problem if you follow the rules listed by Amazon. If you are able to prove that you are sourcing your goods from an authentic source, and follow the guidelines of Amazon,

you would not face any problem in gaining access to these

categories.

Build reputation

The first requirement is that you must be a pro seller. You need to pay a subscription fee monthly to access the Amazon marketplace. The individual sellers of US and basic sellers of UK cannot apply for this. Also, you must have a sales history to build credibility. You can also show your sales history with positive reviews on Amazon FBA.

Have a ready stock of inventory

You must have some inventory ready to sell in the restricted category. Amazon would not wait for you to procure your stock if you are in the process of "thinking" to make sales in the gated categories. They must know that you are a legitimate supplier with geared up inventory. It does not mean that you have to buy huge quantities, but at least a decent amount of stock to show if required. You can even talk to your supplier to negotiate refund policies if you have doubts. If Amazon does not grant permission for the gated categories, you must have some options to sell your goods somewhere else, like on eBay.

Understand other categories individually

All categories have different requirements for approval. Also, Amazon keeps changing the requirements for granting permission to different categories. When the process of application begins, you will get only two days amid each step to submit the information requested by Amazon. You must ensure that you have all your documents in place to avoid delay in submission or cancellation of your application. If you have any doubts, you must contact Seller support beforehand.

Providing images

Some categories require you to submit at least five images of the products to Amazon to gain approval. You can submit images of any of the products but they should comply with the guidelines of Amazon. You do not need to hire a professional photographer to click good photos. You can use any good software to comply with the image guidelines.

Providing invoices

Some categories of products require you to submit the invoices to show that you have bought your goods from a reliable source. Amazon usually requires you to submit three invoices procured from various stores. The invoices should show the name of your business and address, the name, phone number and address of the supplier, quantity bought.

Flat file upload

Some categories require you to submit a flat file of your goods. Flat file implies an Excel Spreadsheet that can be uploaded to the Seller Central so that you can list your products in one go rather than listing them individually. You can procure the templates from Amazon. At least five products are required for this and some of them have to be parent-child goods.

Gaining access to gated categories is not complicated. It is just elaborate. If you comply by the requirements, your process of application will go smoothly.

Other restrictions of Amazon

There are some categories of restricted products which cannot be accessed. It is difficult to get permission for these categories. If you try to make your own listings, you may end up violating Amazon's policies and your account may be blocked. Thus, you must be aware of these strictly restricted categories.

Restricted Brands

Some brands are completely restricted to be sold by other sellers to avoid duplicity or fake products. Some of the examples of such brands include Apple, Burberry and MAC cosmetics. You can list used items of these brands, but not as a new item. Before proceeding for listing restricted products you have doubts about, you must clarify your doubts first. You can even try to contact the brands directly to clarify your doubts.

FBA Restrictions

When you are selling through FBA program of Amazon, you must know about some products which are not allowed to be stored in their warehouse, though you can sell them as an Amazon Merchant. This means that you have to ship them directly from your place.

Some of these products include firearms, razor blades, knives, fireworks, loose gemstones, medicines, etc. In short, anything which is potentially harmful to the warehouse staff cannot be stored at Amazon. But, these restrictions also vary from region to region.

Prohibited Products

Some categories of products are simply not allowed to be sold through Amazon. Some examples are animal products like feathers, fur, ivory, used clothing, e-cigarettes, tobacco products, and of course, live animals.

In brief

You might find many products that are restricted on Amazon. But, in reality, millions products are sold on Amazon. Do not get disheartened if you find the restrictions too elaborate. They are there for your own benefit and of the society at large. You must do the research and ensure that you comprehend the restrictions. If you are not sure about the restrictions on your goods, you can attempt to add it to your account of supplies.

If any listing is associated with your products, Amazon might raise some issues. It is indeed inconvenient. But, you need to take the pain for a few minutes. It will save you the hassle of negotiating refunds from your suppliers.

If there are no listings associated with your products, you can contact the Seller Support to locate any issues linked with your goods.

Chapter 10 Scaling your Amazon FBA Business

In this part, we will discuss how to make an email list for your blog. On the off chance that you converse with any effective blogger, they will reveal to you the significance of having an email list. Having somebody's email will enable you to get in touch with them decisively. It is more probable for individuals to see and tap on your email than it is for them to get some answers concerning your most recent post online which implies you can't neglect the intensity of email and email promoting.

I will show you today how to gather messages through free traffic and pop-ups. Gathering email can be a tedious and an arduous procedure, yet vital.

I will do my best to make it basic for you. Keep in mind that building a decent email rundown will require some serious energy. Additionally, on the grounds that you have figured out how to gather 10,000 messages doesn't mean every one of them will tap on your email.

You have to ensure you are keeping your messages endorsers connected with and hanging tight for the following email, which we will show you in this section. Ultimately, we will additionally manage you on the most proficient method to make probably the most astonishing messages. It will assist you with getting a higher snap through rate. Despite the fact that email showcasing is great, just 30% of individuals will peruse and click your email. We need to ensure we leave no stones unturned to do that and we need an elegantly composed email.

Collecting email

Toward the start of your blogging venture, you won't have a lot of cash to spend on promoting. In this section we will keep everything free assets, which means, you won't need to pay a dime on gathering any messages. Presently there are two fundamental ways for you to acquire messages. The first is through a spring up.

You can utilize email assets like MailChimp to make a free spring up. What spring up will assist you with is the point at which somebody visits your site, they will get a major box directly before them. It will approach them to agree to accept our email list so they could get a free book or something along that line, as we discussed in the past section. Contingent upon your specialty give your readers something of significant worth.

In case you're in the wellness Niche, you can offer your readers free eBooks on the most proficient method to put on muscle. Make sense of the considerable number of requirements and issues individuals have in your specialty. Make a free eBook or a cheat sheet and offer them for nothing. It is an absolute necessity have on your site. Odds are if individuals are on your site as of now, they won't falter to put their email in pop-ups with the expectation of complimentary data.

Your Landing Page

Presently the second method to gather messages is use

something many refer to as a greeting page. When you join with mailchimp.com. which is allowed to utilize, you would then be able to begin making free points of arrival for your site. What presentation page will do is help you gather messages through YouTube and different destinations. In the past section, we discussed gathering messages through YouTube. This is the place points of arrival come in.

Make your presentation page through mailchimp.com. At that point duplicate that connection and post it on your YouTube recordings and different sites on the web. Your presentation page will offer a blessing in return for their email. So in the event that you go on to wellness structures and specialty sites you can gradually include your point of arrival there to explicit individuals who are into your specialty. It is additionally an amazing route for you to gather messages on your YouTube recordings and other specialty related sites. You need your point of arrival there ready for action. On the off chance that not, at that point you are passing up a ton of free leads.

Making email

At long last, the fun part, how to make an email and how regularly you ought to send messages to your readers. So the main thing you have to ensure is that you have your appreciated email computerized. In case you're utilizing the administrations, we prescribe mailchimp.com. You ought to have no issue robotizing email since it is exceptionally direct.

At whatever point somebody agrees to accept your email list, the main thing you have to do is ensure you are sending them the blessing you have guaranteed. Your "appreciated" email will be the main robotized email, ensure your "appreciated" email is sent following they enter their email. This would be your robotized email, since you have made you're free to email and computerized it, we will currently discuss the recurrence and the sorts of email you ought to send your supporters.

As to rate, you ought to never email your readers multiple times each week. There are two explanations behind it. To begin with, you will have a lower possibility of winding up in their spam email. Second, your readers won't get irritated by your messages. Subsequently, they won't withdraw.

With respect to messages, update them about the most recent blog and the partner items you need to offer them two times per week. This is a decent principle guideline I like to live by. Not exclusively will they be locked in on the information you give them, yet they will probably turn into your clients. It won't resemble you're shelled with deals pitch constantly. Subsequent to attempting this for quite a long time and years, I can reveal to you this is the best technique for messaging your readers.

On the off chance that you need to have an effective blog, you need your readers drew in through email. You can lose online networking following, yet the messages will live on until the end of time. Some should seriously think about email medieval, however most organizations are running exclusively on email showcasing. Try not to belittle the intensity of email promoting, particularly for bloggers. Utilize these techniques we just discussed in this section to gather messages. Try not to leave any stones unturned on the off chance that you need to make progress in blogging.

Guest Blogging

As of recently in this book, we have talked about a great deal of approaches to get traffic to your blog. The present part, we're going to discuss the granddaddy of all, visitor blogging. Posting your article on another person's blog, otherwise called visitor blogging is a standout amongst the most ideal ways for you to create traffic to your blog.

Presently there are several things to recall before you begin posting your online journals on other individuals' sites. The main thing you need to ensure is that you have a few online journals all alone website before you post on others. Let's be honest, nobody needs new bloggers to post on their site, get a few certifications and compose an incredible blog or two develop a resume. When you've figured out how to post two or three online journals all alone website, at that point you can begin reviewing visitor writes so as to create more traffic and to get some reputation in your specialty.

The sooner you begin visitor blogging, the better it will be for your image. It will enable you to make more backlinks, however it will likewise enable you to draw in more readers to your blog. Another extraordinary thing about this strategy is that if the site you posted on gets new readers, the odds of the new readers to visit and turn into a reader of your blog would be exceptionally high. Presently you should simply discover individuals who will enable you to post on their site, that is the thing that we will show you in this section.

Be precise with your niche

Before we move further into this section, we have to clear up two or three things. On the off chance that you need to take advantage of your visitor blogging attempts, at that point you have to ensure that the site which you have chosen to visitor present on is connected on your specialty. It can't be "kind of" related with your specialty, it must be unequivocally identified with your specialty.

For example, in the event that your specialty is tied in with weight training, at that point you discover a yoga site searching for a visitor blogger, don't proceed to attempt and post on their website as you won't increase any traffic from it. Kindly remember this progression as it is basic for your achievement in the blogging scene. You won't win any new readers from it. On the off chance that the "kind of" related site chooses to post your article on their site, they may lose a few readers and you may likewise lose a ton of regard in the blogging scene.

Discovering sites to post on

Before you feel free to discover locales to post on, ensure that the site you find is progressing nicely. The most ideal approach to see whether the sites are getting a ton of connected readers is to perceive what number of social offers a particular article or the site is getting.

That is a standout amongst the most ideal approaches to see whether the site is a go-go or no-go. Beyond any doubt you can post it on every one of the spots conceivable yet this will just make you look frantic for traffic That isn't what you need to look like in case you will have a long haul continued business.

Presently there are a great deal of approaches to discover sites to post on, however the best site is clearly Google.

Simply look "Present a visitor post." If you see a site in your specialty which is tolerating visitor posts, email them. It is as basic as it sounds. They may request that you send a connection to your ongoing post so ensure you are composing the most ideal articles.

Composing the post

When you at long last found your site to post your blog on and they have acknowledged you, it will be a great opportunity to compose the article. Contingent upon the webpage and their readers, your composing must be at a similar dimension as the site you will be visitor blogging on. This will enable you to pull in more readers to your blog.

So as to do that, you have to do explore about their site. Peruse every one of the articles you can on their site. At that point make sense of if their perusers are propelled level, apprentices or transitional. Since that will have a major effect in the rush hour gridlock, you will create from your visitor post.

You would prefer not to compose a careful article on a learner's site. It will just make readers neglect your articles. Generally speaking ensure that you are obliging their gathering of people. Which means, you need to compose a fundamental article if their site is an essential site and the other way around.

Discover what is working

When you are doing your examination on the site, attempt to

discover the most shared and the most seen post. That will enable you to make sense of what the group of onlookers needs. Attempt and compose a comparative post simply like the most prevalent one on their site. That will fulfill the site as they would get a great deal of perspectives and offers. Likewise, this will help you hugely support your blog subsequently developing your business.

Keep in mind, when you have the chance to compose on another person's blog, it isn't about you or your image. You are composing as a visitor, helping the site get more perspectives and offers. Visitor blogging will enable you to produce more traffic to your blog, however that ought not be your essential core interest.

In the event that you attempt and advance yourself in the visitor post, at that point odds of you landing more positions later on will be practically nothing. Trust me, you will get traffic from visitor posting yet don't advance yourself on the article. That being stated, I trust you have delighted in this book so far as we are arriving at its finish. The last two parts will tell you the best way to take your blog past the $10,000 a month point we have been discussing in this book.

By now you should have your product listing page built and your products on the way to the fulfillment center or waiting there ready to be sold! In this section I will be covering the most effective ways that you can start driving traffic to your product to make your initial sales. It's time to start making money!

Facebook and Instagram ads

Currently, both Facebook and Instagram are the most used social media platforms. This means that there is a great chance that your prospects are there. If properly done, you can generate traffic from there down to your website. You can convert the traffic to clients, who want to click more, watch your videos, and install your mobile apps.

Getting these results are possible, but you have to put efforts into it.

Facebook and Instagram Ads work together. You don't have to create an Instagram account before you can craft out an Instagram Ad. You can make use of your Facebook account. The option can be accessed in the settings of the account.

That's not all, as these social media channels permit you to reduce how much you spend on marketing, as your ads can easily be targeted to the right audience.

Let's say; you are promoting a dirt bike; you can easily have your Facebook and Instagram are targeted to those that are lovers of dirt bikes and their accessories.

One thing that a lot of marketers love about both ads is the fact that their targeting options are well defined. This means that you can choose whomever you want your product targeted to.

Instagram and Facebook are social networks, where people try to have fun, hence whatever you do there should be tailored to make their lives fun. No one will leave a fun activity to stare at a boring ad. A smart affiliate knows how to tailor their ads to capture the attention of their targeted audience.

Since Instagram and Facebook have a lot of targeting options, they allow businesses to reach their prospects by putting the ads on either the Instagram stories or newsfeed. This prevents the ads from coming off as being out of place.

CONCLUSION

In the end you will have realized that the advantage is obvious: the company is disconnected from traditional logistics, including ecommerce.

Using Amazon FBA allows you to eliminate overhead fixed costs: in this way you can focus only on the sourcing part:

• Find the right product (Product Search)

• Finding the right manufacturer (there are thousands of them in China)

• Import it correctly

The Amazon FBA business allows thousands of people every day to earn a nice nest egg and live their lives in peace, from the comfort of their own home.

We also wish you the same thing, to find your size, to find the right product for you and to make the most of this business to achieve your goals !!

CPSIA information can be obtained
at www.ICGtesting.com
Printed in the USA
BVHW061416250221
601119BV00001B/36